S0-BXW-254

DEMCO

The Old English Sheepdog

by William R. Sanford and Carl R. Green

New York

CIP

LIBRARY OF CONGRESS CATALOGING IN PUBLICATION DATA

Sanford, William R. (William Reynolds)
  Old English sheepdog

  (Top dog)
  Includes index.
  SUMMARY: Discusses the history, physical characteristics, care, and breeding of this
large dog bred to work with sheep and cattle.
  1. Old English sheepdog — Juvenile literature. [1. Old English sheepdog. 2. Dogs.] I.
Green, Carl R. II. Title. III. Series: Sanford, William R. (William Reynolds), Top dog.
SF429.O4S36   1989   636.7'37 — dc20   89-31073
ISBN 0-89686-452-9

◤ PHOTO CREDITS

Cover: Reynolds Photography: Larry Reynolds
Reynolds Photography: (Larry Reynolds) 43
Photo Researchers, Inc.: (John Henry Sullivan, Jr.) 4; (Farrell
  Grehan) 6; (E. Vogeler) 21
Photri: 10; (B. Kulik) 29, 32
FPG International: (K. Haynes) 13; (Larry Grant) 17, 27, 30;
  (G. Marche) 19; (Angelo Giampiccolo) 45
American Stock Photography: 35
Third Coast Stock Source: (J. P. Slatter) 38

Macmillan Publishing Company
866 Third Avenue
New York, NY 10022
Collier Macmillan Canada, Inc.

CRESTWOOD HOUSE

Produced by Carnival Enterprises

Printed in the United States of America

First Edition

10   9   8   7   6   5   4   3   2   1

TABLE OF CONTENTS

FOR MORE INFORMATION

For more information about Old English sheepdogs, write to:

American Kennel Club
51 Madison Avenue
New York, NY 10010

Old English Sheepdog Club
185 Coriell Avenue
Fanwood, NJ 07023

BONNIE BLUE

Leslie Ann heard her father calling, but she didn't answer right away. She hurried to finish the postcard she was writing.

"Tammy, this trip to England is the greatest!" she wrote. "London was exciting, but staying here in the Yorkshire Dales is even better. My Uncle Harold has a sheep farm, and he's been super to us. Best of all, I have a new boyfriend! He has long, shaggy hair and soft brown eyes. His name is Bonnie Blue... and (fooled you!) he's an Old Engish sheepdog. Most days, we go for long walks together. Today, though, I'm going to watch Blue drive the sheep to market. Love, Leslie Ann."

Leslie ran down the creaky stairs. Her dad and Uncle Harold were waiting in the farmyard. Blue saw her and came bounding up. Leslie smiled as she patted his broad head. She wondered again how Blue could see through the hair that covered his eyes.

"It's market day in Hawes," Uncle Harold said. "This is Blue's favorite job. He loves to drive the sheep to town."

Dark gray clouds were moving across the quiet valley. "We'd better get started before the rains come," Leslie said.

A mass of long hair covers the head of the friendly Old English sheepdog.

5

Harold led the way past the gray stone barns. The dog ran ahead to the gate that led into the fields. "Blue knows that it's market day," he said with a smile. "I don't have to tell him."

Leslie unhooked the gate and swung it open. Blue looked at Harold, waiting for a command. When the farmer made sweeping motions with his hands, Blue broke into a fast trot. The sheepdog often looked clumsy when he was clowning around. Now, he was all business as he shifted into an easy, graceful trot.

Blue headed toward a dozen sheep that were grazing at the far end of the field. When he

A well-trained Old English sheepdog will respond quickly to its owner's hand signals.

reached them, he looked back. The farmer whistled and made a circling motion with his right hand.

"Does Blue understand all those signals?" Leslie asked.

"You can be sure he does," her uncle replied. He watched Blue closely as he talked. The dog was driving the unhappy sheep into a small circle. "At this distance he can hear my voice. If he's farther away, my whistle will reach him. In a storm, when he can't hear me at all, he responds to my arm signals."

Blue seemed to be everywhere at once. If a sheep stepped out of line, the sheepdog was there to nip at its heels. Without fuss and without barking, Blue drove his woolly flock through the gate.

As the sheep started down the lane, Blue cut left and vanished behind the barn. "Watch this, Leslie," Harold said. "Blue's done this a thousand times. He knows what the sheep are going to do before they know it themselves."

As they rounded the barn, the sheep spread out. An old ram and two ewes headed for the watering trough. They never reached it, because Blue was waiting for them. The dog quickly drove the sheep back to the lane. Moments later, the entire flock was heading toward the main road to town. The ram was bleating a loud protest, but he didn't try to stray again.

Leslie held her uncle's hand as they walked. "Uncle Harold," she said, "Blue's a lot smarter than I thought he was." She looked up. "Now, I'd like to know more about the Old English sheepdog."

HISTORY OF THE OLD ENGLISH SHEEPDOG

Like all other dogs, Old English sheepdogs are meat-eating mammals. They belong to the scientific order *Carnivora*. Dogs, jackals, wolves, and foxes are in the family known as the *Canidae*. Every *domestic dog*, large or small, belongs to the same species, *Canis familiaris*.

Thanks to careful *breeding*, there are hundreds of different breeds of dog. Some breeds, such as the greyhound, have been with us for thousands of years. Other breeds, such as the toy poodle, are quite new. What about the Old English sheepdog? The word "old" suggests that it has been around for a long time. Not so. The breed has existed for only about 200 years.

The Old English sheepdog was developed by sheep farmers. They didn't care about *pedigrees*. All they wanted was a strong working dog that was good with sheep and cattle. In Scotland, the collie filled that need. In southern England, the Old English sheepdog did the job.

No one knows exactly what breeds were *crossbred* to produce the Old English sheepdog. The Russian Owtchah, for example, looks like an oversized Old English sheepdog. Of today's breeds, the British bearded collie is clearly a close cousin.

The breed developed in the early 1800s. The place was England's western counties of Devon, Somerset, and Cornwall. The dogs were used mostly as drovers. Their job was to drive sheep and cattle from one place to another. The custom of cutting off, or *docking*, the sheepdog's tail also started at that time. In order to evade the tax on long-tailed hunting dogs, owners had to prove that their sheepdogs were working dogs. Thus, they docked their dogs' tails. No tail, no tax! The

The "bobtail" is a popular nickname for Old English sheepdogs because their tails are docked when they are puppies.

custom gave the Old English sheepdog a popular nickname: the bobtail.

The first Old English sheepdog was registered in the United States in 1886. By then, breeders were developing the Old English as a *show dog*. Standards for the breed were drawn up. In a collie show held in 1899, Old English sheepdogs won most of the prizes! The breed grew even more popular after 1903. That was the year Bouncing Lass won top honors at a big Westminster Show. In 1987, these shaggy dogs were 42nd on the list of popular breeds.

A CLOSE LOOK AT THE OLD ENGLISH SHEEPDOG

"What a funny dog. She looks just like a teddy bear!"

The owners of Old English sheepdogs are used to that comment. These big, shaggy dogs do look like stuffed, roly-poly toys.

Despite their looks, Old English sheepdogs are large, strong dogs. A male measures upward of 22 inches at the *withers* (the top of the shoulder). A show-quality dog should be about as long as it is tall. An adult male weighs from 85 to 100 pounds. Females are a little shorter and weigh about 20 pounds less. Dog show standards discourage the showing of dogs taller than 26 inches.

The Old English sheepdog's heavy coat gives it the teddy bear look. The long, shaggy coat comes in shades of gray, blue-gray, or blue-black. Brown markings are not acceptable at dog shows. Large areas of white on the head, chest, and legs are common. The long outer

11

coat covers a thick, woolly undercoat. Cold, wet weather doesn't bother the bobtail!

It may look roly-poly, but the Old English is a powerful, heavy-boned animal. The head is large and the skull is well rounded. A large black nose sticks out of the mass of long hair that covers the head. Lift the hair and you'll see dark brown eyes. China blue eyes are fairly common, but dark eyes are preferred. The neck is long and arched, the body short and compact. The forelegs are straight, the hindlegs round and muscular. A sheepdog's back slopes down slightly from its rump to its withers. According to custom, *puppies* still have their tails docked soon after they're born.

Like all dogs, the Old English sheepdog's teeth are those of a meat eater, or *carnivore*. The puppy begins to lose its baby teeth in the fourth month. Three months later, all 42 adult teeth will be in place. The three types of teeth are shaped for special tasks. In the front of the mouth are 12 *incisors*, or biting teeth. Next to them are 4 powerful *canines*, used for tearing. Farther back in the jaw are 26 *molars* and *premolars*. These heavy teeth are used for chewing and crushing. An Old English that's fed properly shouldn't develop bad teeth, but gum disease is sometimes a problem. Dogs

Although it may look roly-poly, the Old English sheepdog is a powerful animal.

that chew on too many bones can wear their teeth down to useless stubs.

No puppy ever heard the advice, "Chew your food or you'll get a stomachache!" If a chunk of meat is small enough for the puppy to swallow, down it goes. The dog's throat expands to four or five times normal size to let food pass through. Digestion begins in the stomach, where strong acids attack the unchewed food.

KEEN SENSES

Dog experts say the Old English sheepdog is one of the smartest of all dogs. When working on a farm, for example, it easily outthinks the slow-witted sheep and cows. This hardworking breed learns commands quickly and follows them exactly.

There is a limit to the sheepdog's abilities, however. The human brain, for example, weighs around three pounds. In a 90-pound dog, the brain weighs only about five ounces. That means there isn't much room for high-level thinking in a dog's brain. The brain is mostly occupied by the tasks of seeing, hearing, and smelling. Taste and touch are not important senses to a dog.

A sheepdog's eyes are similar to a human's eyes in many ways. If sheepdogs have any vision problems, it's because their eyes are half-covered by fringes of hair. Although sheepdogs are color-blind, they see a wider field of vision than people do. They also have better night vision and a third, protective eyelid called the *haw*. Unlike humans, Old English sheepdogs see things in motion better than things that aren't moving. Imagine that a rabbit is sitting downwind of your dog, 50 yards away. As long as it doesn't move, the rabbit looks like a small mound of earth. One tiny movement, however, will catch the dog's attention. Then the chase begins.

All Old English sheepdogs are born with blue eyes. If the adult dog is going to have brown eyes, the darker color will show up at about six weeks of age. In older dogs, cataracts sometimes form on the lenses of the eyes. The cataracts cloud the lenses and can cause blindness. *Veterinarians* can correct most cataracts if treatment starts early enough.

An Old English sheepdog's hearing is better than yours in three ways. A dog can hear higher tones, detect fainter sounds, and locate the source of a sound more accurately. If a high-pitched sound goes over 20,000 cycles a second, humans can't hear it. Dogs can, and that's why they can hear a "silent" dog whistle. An Old English makes about 20 different barks, growls, whines, and howls. If you listen carefully to the dog's deep voice, you can learn the meaning of many of them.

Like its hearing, the sheepdog's sense of smell is amazingly keen. Dogs have much larger *olfactory patches* in their noses than humans do. As they breathe, the air reports a rainbow of scents to them. A sheepdog can detect one part urine in 60 million parts of water! Since each dog marks its territory with urine, other dogs can easily "read" the message that's been left. That's why your dog spends so much time sniffing when it's out for a walk.

If you enter your dog in an *obedience trial,* it will have to use its nose. During one test, you'll be asked to handle a small wooden object. A judge will place that object beside a dozen others that you haven't touched. Your dog's task is to fetch the object that carries your scent. Old English sheepdogs think this is a wonderful game.

A STRONG PERSONALITY

Do you dislike big, hairy dogs? Do you prefer dogs that have weak personalities? If the answer is yes to either question, don't buy an Old English sheepdog!

The Old English sheepdog's size and shaggy coat are easy to see. What doesn't show is the dog's big heart. Sheepdogs are loving, protective, and brave. They don't look for fights, but they'll defend their "flock" to the death. A breeder named Goodsell found that out when

Old English sheepdogs are loving, protective, and brave.

he took a sheepdog named Marksman for a walk. Goodsell was strolling with Marksman, a neighbor's child, and two puppies. Suddenly, a German shepherd jumped a wall and ran at them. Instantly, Marksman threw himself on the attacker. As Goodsell pulled the child and the puppies to safety, Marksman killed the other dog. Old English sheepdogs may look slow and clumsy, but don't be fooled. They are serious guard dogs.

On the other side of the coin, Old English sheepdogs are full of fun and mischief. The minute you finish *grooming* your pet, it will start clowning around. Ten minutes later, it will look like an unmade bed. Remember, too, that the breed earned the name *sheepdog* honestly. The dog's herding *instincts* run deep. It's quite common to see a sheepdog herding chickens, ducks, and children. A young dog may even nip its owner while trying to keep the family "herd" in line.

This herding instinct means that Old English sheepdogs are wonderful baby-sitters. Parents can relax when their sheepdog is on guard. Little kids can climb all over their playmate without hurting it. At the same time, the dog is always ready to protect its "flock."

Old English sheepdogs aren't for everyone. For one thing, they're at their best in the country. Keeping a large, active dog in the big city is hard on both dog and owner. The Old English needs more care than busy city people can give it. It demands attention and lots of exercise. If these big, hairy dogs aren't given the spotlight, they sometimes misbehave. In addition, that handsome coat needs constant care. Let it go too long, and it will turn into a tangled, matted mess. Worst of all, a neglected dog can lose its sweet nature.

On the plus side, an Old English sheepdog is a natural homebody. Even with the gate open,

18

A good run is healthy for dogs and their owners.

your dog isn't likely to wander away. If a strange dog wanders by, the Old English won't pick a fight. It won't back away from one, either! Within its human family, the Old English is a "one-person" dog. That's usually the child or adult who feeds, trains, and plays with it.

CHOOSING A PUPPY

You've decided that you can't live without an Old English sheepdog. What's next? Here are

the most popular questions asked by buyers—
and the experts' answers:

Where can I find a good-quality puppy?
Finding a seller you can trust is an important
step. Honest breeders and pet-store owners
guarantee their dogs. They won't sell you a
diseased or bad-tempered puppy. You can locate them by looking in dog magazines or by
asking your local veterinarian to help. If you
buy from a breeder, you should see the puppy's mother and some of its brothers and sis-
ters. The adult dogs will give you an idea of
what your puppy will be like when it's grown.
By contrast, a pet store may have only a single puppy to show you.

Can sheepdogs be show dogs? The decision to
buy an Old English sheepdog of show quality
is a big one. Show dogs cost more and require
more care. You'll need help in choosing one,
because a show dog must meet the highest
standards set for the breed. A show-quality
dog will cost from $400 to $500. A pet-quality
dog costs from $250 to $300. Buying a less expensive dog doesn't mean you're getting second best. A pet-quality Old English lacks only
the perfection that wins blue ribbons.

How do I know the puppy is healthy? A
healthy puppy will be alert, playful, and clean.

A show-quality sheepdog will cost between $400 and $500.

Never buy a puppy that has cloudy eyes, a swollen belly, or a runny nose. Ask the breeder if the parents were checked for *hip dysplasia*. This is a crippling condition that doesn't show up until the puppy is six months to one year old. If your dog develops this condition, a good breeder will replace it with another puppy or return your money. Just as you reject puppies that are too shy or too aggressive, watch out for "spinners." These are puppies that have been cooped up in tiny cages.

21

When let out, they spin around in crazy circles. Ask the seller for the puppy's health record, including its shots. Once you buy your dog, take it to a vet for an exam. If it fails the checkup, return it to the seller.

Why should I pay extra for a purebred? If you're in love with Old English sheepdogs, you'll want a *purebred*. Purebred dogs inherit the looks and behaviors of their breed. A purebred puppy comes with a pedigree that lists its ancestors. Once you have the papers in hand, register your dog with a national kennel club. This protects the value of the pups if you decide to breed your Old English. Show dogs should also be registered.

Should I buy a male or a female puppy? Most people choose a female, even though males are a little cheaper. The female makes a better house dog, and she's usually smaller than the male. As a bonus, the female can be bred if you want to raise puppies. Twice a year a female is ready to mate and have puppies. This is known as coming into *heat*. If you don't want her to mate, you'll have to keep her away from male dogs at that time.

What age should my puppy be? An Old English sheepdog is ready to go home with you as early as six weeks after it's born. Most breeders think that's too early and prefer nine to ten weeks. By that time, it's easy to judge a puppy's personality. Also, an older puppy is fully *weaned* (doesn't nurse anymore), has had its puppy shots, and has been checked for *worms*. Frisky and anxious to please you, the puppy is ready for training.

TRAINING AN OLD ENGLISH SHEEPDOG

Old English sheepdogs are lovely, playful pets. They're also mischievous and stubborn. If an Old English isn't well trained, it can be difficult to control. Being jumped on by a 90-pound dog is like being hit by a small elephant!

Good breeders begin the training process early. They handle the puppies and play with them. By the time you pick your puppy from the *litter*, it should be used to people. Remember that your new puppy is not a four-legged human being. It's a dog, and it's driven by instincts.

The first goal of most owners is to *housebreak* their dog. No one wants a puppy that soils the living room carpet. One good thing is that the Old English sheepdog won't soil its own sleeping place. Your dog will want to use another spot to relieve itself. Your job is to help it choose the proper place.

Some owners of Old English sheepdogs have good luck with the "crate method." They house their puppies in wooden crates that are just big enough for comfort. If you keep your puppy in a crate, it'll think that's home. Since it then won't want to soil the crate, you can control the times it relieves itself. Later, if you travel with it, it won't mind being shut up in a crate.

Your dog will usually relieve itself after eating. Feed it at the same time every day. Then take it outside to the spot you want it to use. The odors it leaves there will encourage it to use the same spot again. Don't take it out of the crate unless someone is watching it. Letting a puppy run loose in the house usually ends in disaster.

If you see your dog make a mistake, let it know it was wrong. Scold it while you hold its nose close to the mess. Then take it outside. Afterward, wash the area to remove any odor from the spot. If you don't catch your dog "in the act," forget the scolding. Your dog won't understand why it's being punished. When it performs properly, praise it and pet it. Your dog lives for your praise, and it'll work to earn more of it.

Every new step in your dog's training should follow the same rules. Be patient and be consistent. Always use your dog's name when you talk to it. If it jumps up on you, say, for example, "Down, Misty!" as you push it down. Don't let it jump one day and then scold it the next. *Reinforce* the lessons with dog biscuits. Dogs are greedy animals. Once a dog knows that it can earn a treat by obeying you, it will work even harder.

If you live in the city, your dog will need daily walks. Always take it out on a leash. The best training leash is a chain made of heavy metal links, called a *choke chain*. When you pull back on it, the chain cuts off the dog's air. As soon as it responds, release the pressure. Your dog will quickly learn to obey when you say, "Stay!" Without the choke chain, your dog will soon be dragging you wherever it wants to go.

Your dog will have many more lessons to learn. If you need help, take it to dog obedience school. The class will help you turn an unruly puppy into a calm, well-behaved pet.

CARING FOR YOUR OLD ENGLISH SHEEPDOG

There are four keys to keeping an Old English sheepdog healthy: good diet, regular visits to the vet, exercise, and proper grooming.

Like all dogs, the Old English sheepdog needs a balanced diet that's heavy on proteins. Instead of cooking up special meals, many breeders use packaged dog food. Dry food comes in many forms, from a gritty meal to large biscuits. Puppies do well on a diet of dry food, cow's milk, and a little extra meat. Some owners don't trust the prepared foods. They give their dogs ground beef, cow's milk, brown bread, and extra vitamins. Always keep a dish of fresh water where the dog can get to it.

A new puppy eats five times a day. By four months, you can cut the feedings to three a day. Two meals are enough for a nine-month-old dog. Puppies graduate to adulthood at one year, when they can get by on one meal a day.

To stay healthy, sheepdogs need a good diet, exercise, grooming, and regular visits to a vet.

Here's a typical diet for a large three-year-old: five cups of dry food, one pound of ground beef, a little coconut oil, and some multipurpose vitamins. Feeding an Old English isn't cheap!

A dog should be slightly hungry after each meal. Given all the food it wants, an Old English will soon grow fat and lazy. In addition, most of them are beggars. If you give in and feed yours with extra tidbits, it may refuse its regular diet. Above all, never give fish or chicken bones to your dog. A dog can choke to death on small bones. Dogs love sweets, but candy will cause cavities. For a treat, give your dog a milkbone now and then. These tough "bones" exercise the jaws and help keep the dog's teeth clean.

Most experts say Old English sheepdogs should sleep outdoors. With their heavy coats, they don't mind the cold. Fix up a sturdy, rainproof doghouse in a corner that's out of the wind. If that's not possible, an unheated porch is okay. The dog doesn't need a special bed. Your Old English will be happy with a blanket and some shredded newspaper. Dogs do catch cold, so make sure yours isn't sleeping in a draft.

Your new puppy must have a series of "puppy shots." The shots guard the dog from *distemper* and other serious diseases. Your vet can also check for worms and for hip dysplasia.

Old English sheepdogs must have plenty of exercise. A dog that has a big yard to run in will probably keep itself in good condition. Otherwise, you'll have to go for lots of fast walks. Figure on a minimum of three miles a day. It's fun to vary the walking with a fast

A sturdy, rainproof doghouse makes an excellent outdoor home for an Old English sheepdog.

game of fetch. When the exercise is over, it's time to groom your shaggy friend. As you can see, owning an Old English isn't for couch potatoes!

KEEPING A SHEEPDOG GROOMED

Owners of Old English sheepdogs love to hear friends say, "Oh, what a lovely coat your dog has!" Indeed, that smooth, thick hair is

Although most sheepdogs need only a weekly brushing to look good, show dogs need daily grooming.

one of the breed's chief glories. Keeping the coat in good condition isn't easy. Left untended, the hair will tangle itself into an ugly mat. If the matted coat isn't brushed at once, the dog's coat may have to be clipped.

Breeders know that some sheepdogs are more likely to mat than others. Those that mat badly may need up to 30 minutes of grooming every day. The same is true of show dogs. Other dogs need only a weekly brushing. If you go away on vacation, someone else should do the grooming. Otherwise, your dog will look like a messy doormat by the time you come home.

Most groomers use a brush. Always start at the bottom of your pet's legs and work upward. Hold your dog's unbrushed hair out of the way with your free hand. As you brush, you'll undo many tangles. Clearing a tangle in the coarse outer coat will pull out a bit of the fleecy undercoat. Don't worry; there's plenty more where that came from. Do the hind legs first, then the forelegs. Next, work back from the withers to the rump. Finally, do the dog's head. A well-trained dog will sit quietly for its brushing. If you save your dog's "wool," you can make good use of it. Some owners have it woven into warm gloves or scarves.

While you're grooming your dog, check its ears, paws, and skin. Long-haired dogs often develop an ear disease called *canker*. You can protect your dog by cleaning its ears once a week. In the same way, clean away the hair balls and dried mud that collect between its toes. Mucous sometimes dries at the corners of its eyes, so swab that away, too. If your dog has been scratching, it may have fleas or it may be developing a *hot spot*. Treat fleas with powders and a flea collar. A hot spot shows up as a red, raw area on the dog's skin. A vet can tell you the proper way to treat it.

Unless your dog has been chasing skunks or rolling in dirt, it won't need many baths. If you must bathe it, ask for help! It will take two or more of you to hold your dog as it scrambles around in a slippery bathtub. Afterward, allow plenty of time for drying its coat. It might catch a chill if it goes outdoors in cold weather before it's fully dry.

Finally, your dog is perfectly groomed. It's

During the hot summer months, some owners clip their sheepdogs' hair close. They know the hair will grow back in time for winter.

beautiful! If it's a female, you might begin to think that she'd be a good mother. Maybe you could breed her, raise the puppies, and sell them.

BREEDING AND RAISING PUPPIES

If you own a purebred female dog, you don't want puppies to just happen. The process of mating your Old English sheepdog to a good male is called breeding.

A *bitch*, as breeders call the female dog, should be at least one year old before you breed her. If she's over four years old, she may be too old. In any case, have her checked by a vet before you begin. Good breeders go a step further. They never breed a dog that has a serious flaw of any kind.

Most breeders keep a champion male *stud*. By mating two dogs of show quality, they're more likely to get fine puppies. The cost of mating your female is called a stud fee. Most people pay the fee by letting the stud's owner take "the pick of the litter." If your female doesn't become pregnant, the breeder will let you bring her back a second time.

Once the bitch is pregnant, nature will take over. Old English sheepdog puppies are born nine weeks after the female is mated. During that time, she will need special care. Give her a high-protein diet and lots of gentle exercise. At the seven-week mark, clip the hair on her rump and belly. This prevents infection and makes it easier for the puppies to suckle. Finally, set aside a warm, quiet place for the *whelping*, or birth.

Sheepdogs are good mothers and usually give birth with little trouble. Most litters have eight to ten puppies. Each puppy emerges headfirst, covered in its birth sac. After the female helps it break the sac, she bites through the *umbilical cord*. Next, she licks the puppy to clean and warm it. It may take six to twelve hours for the whole litter to arrive. Old English sheepdog puppies weigh as much as one pound at birth. They're born deaf and their eyes are closed, but they'll be nursing within the first two hours.

A veterinarian will dock the puppies' tails on the third day. Because the entire tail is removed, this must be done with great care. The vet can also remove *dewclaws* at this time.

Old English sheepdog puppies grow quickly. At ten days their eyes open, and at two weeks they are able to walk on wobbly legs.

These are the useless claws that sometimes grow on the inside of a dog's hind legs. The vet will tell you if the puppies need extra food. In most cases, the female's milk is enough. After all, her milk is 12 percent fat, compared to the 3.7 percent in cow's milk.

An Old English sheepdog puppy grows quickly. In a year, it will increase its weight up to 80 times! At ten days, the puppy's eyes will open. By two weeks, it will be able to walk on wobbly legs. The female will begin weaning the puppies after four weeks. You can let the puppies lick milk from your fingers to help them learn to drink from a pan. By six weeks, they should be weaned. Two weeks later, they'll be ready to go to new homes.

If you're lucky, you'll find buyers who will pay a good price for your puppies. Even if that happens, you may not make any money. The vet's fees are expensive. Also, there's the cost of feeding hungry puppies after they're weaned. Most breeders who raise sheepdogs do so because they love them. They're happy if they break even at the end of the year.

SHOWING YOUR OLD ENGLISH SHEEPDOG

Joan has just finished a fast game of tag with Magic, her Old English sheepdog. As Joan grooms him, she can't help thinking he's beautiful. Besides, his papers prove that he comes from a race of champions. On his pedigree, or list of ancestors, his formal name is White Magic of Derrydown.

Then a thought strikes Joan. "There's a big dog show at the armory next month. Magic and I will show this town what a *real* Old English sheepdog looks like!"

When Joan calls the armory, she learns that this will be licensed show. The winners will earn points toward an American Kennel Club championship. Next, Joan is told that it will be for all breeds. That means the dogs will be divided into six groups: sporting, hound, working, terrier, toy, and nonsporting. Sheepdogs belong in the working dog group.

Joan's long-term goal is to see Magic crowned as a champion, the Best of Breed and the Best of Show. But in his first show, he can't be both of those. First, he must win 15 points in order to be called a champion (Ch.). Then, as Ch. White Magic of Derrydown, he can compete for the top prizes. The most Magic can win at this show is five points. It takes at least three big shows to win a championship.

Grooming Magic to look good for the show isn't Joan's only task. With all those people and dogs around him, Magic must stay calm. Joan practices the obedience commands. She makes sure he will stand quietly by her side no matter what happens. When the judging starts, Magic must parade slowly around the

An Old English sheepdog keeps its head up as it and other dogs walk around the ring for the judges.

ring with the other dogs. Joan trains him to walk with only a loose lead, but makes sure he keeps his head up. Joan lets him know there's a tidbit in her pocket, so he'll always be watching her hand.

Joan arrives at the show early so Magic can get used to the noise and the smells. Joan watches the other handlers when they show their dogs. Many good dogs have lost because their handlers didn't know how to show them. About 30 minutes before Magic's class is called, Joan gives him some exercise. Then she takes care of his final grooming. Joan wants to deliver Magic to the ring with every hair in place.

Finally, the announcer calls Magic's class to the ring. Joan takes her place with the other handlers. She parades Magic around the ring at a slow *gait* with the other owners. The judges look at each dog. When it's Joan's turn, the judges examine Magic carefully. Magic stands quietly while the judges check him from nose to tail. Afterward, Joan leads Magic back to the side of the ring. It's a tense moment as Joan waits for the judge's decision.

For all Joan's careful work, Magic doesn't win a prize. There are lots of shows, however, and Joan will learn something each time she enters. Maybe the next show will send Joan home with a blue ribbon!

WHY DOES A SHEEPDOG PANT SO MUCH?

Every evening, Jimmy Meyer takes his Old English sheepdog out for a run. The exercise is harder on Jimmy than it is on Alpha. Even when Jimmy sprints, Alpha lopes easily beside him. She looks shaggy and awkward, but she's very fast. Off the leash, she can outrun the fastest Olympic sprinter.

At the end of the run, both Jimmy and Alpha are breathing hard. Jimmy leans forward, gasping for air. Alpha pants right along with him. Her mouth is open and her long tongue is hanging out. Jimmy soon catches his breath, but the dog is still breathing fast. "Why are you panting?" Jimmy asks her. "You weren't working hard. I don't think you even broke a sweat."

Sweat, the dog experts say, is what a dog's panting is all about. People sweat when they're hot. The trickles of sweat evaporate and help to cool our bodies. Alpha, like all other dogs, doesn't have sweat glands. When the first dogs were evolving, they were heavily furred. So even if these dogs did have sweat glands, they were useless. In time, the ability to sweat was lost.

The loss of sweat glands created a problem. A dog will die if it becomes overheated. Alpha has a normal body temperature of 101.5 degrees Fahrenheit. On a hot day, if she runs too much, her temperature may go up to 104 degrees Fahrenheit. If she can't reduce her body heat, she'll die of heatstroke. That's where panting comes in.

By panting, Alpha speeds up the cooling process. As she breathes in and out, her tongue serves as a radiator. The air cools the blood in her tongue, and her heart pumps the cooler blood to her body. When she's hot, Alpha will also drink more water than usual. This makes up for the water lost in the cooling process. Under normal conditions, panting brings the dog's body heat down quickly. Alpha has long hair, but shorthaired and hairless dogs cool off in the same way. Even on the hottest day, the skin of a Mexican hairless feels dry to the touch.

Once in a while, a dog will pant even though it hasn't been exercising. That's a sure sign the dog is overheated. In most cases, moving the animal into a cooler place will solve the problem. At the same time, be sure it has plenty of water to drink. If the dog's temperature is very high, place it in a bath of cool water. After it has recovered, dry it off so that it won't become chilled.

Every summer, many dogs die when careless owners leave them locked in hot cars. With the sun beating in, the temperature may rise to 120 degrees Fahrenheit or more. Trapped in the car, the dog gets hotter and hotter. By the time the owner returns, the dog may be dead from heatstroke. In the oven heat of a car, panting doesn't help very much.

On the walk home, Alpha's breathing soon returns to normal. Jimmy doesn't have to worry about her. Her sheepdog ancestors had to do a lot more running than she does.

BARNABY, THE SUPERSTAR SHEEPDOG

Like many young stars, Barnaby got his big break when an older actor became ill.

For many years, Patrick was the top Old English sheepdog in New York. He acted in commercials and on television. Patrick worked for his owner and trainer, Barbara Austin. The two were both friends and business partners.

A few days before filming a dog food commercial, Patrick came down with a serious stomach problem. He was 12 years old, the equal of an 80-year-old human. Dr. Milts saved Patrick's life, but his acting days were over.

It happened that Dr. Milts owned a fine Old English sheepdog named Barnaby. Barnaby

When a dog gets overheated or runs, it pants to cool itself down.

was beautiful and obedient. Well, Barnaby was obedient most of the time. In his eagerness to be the center of attention, he sometimes overdid things. Even so, Barbara decided to give him a tryout.

On his first film set, Barnaby was in heaven. He made friends with the crew and gobbled down the sponsor's dog food. Barbara did her best to control him, but Barnaby ignored her. The film director was angry. How could he film a commercial with a dog who wouldn't follow the script?

Luckily for Barbara, the sponsor was there that day. The man liked the dog's happy-go-lucky style. Instead of firing Barnaby, he told the director to rewrite the script. "Just do whatever the dog is doing," he ordered.

A popular commercial came out of the madhouse that followed. During Barnaby's 30 seconds on camera, he chases a tiny covered wagon across a slippery kitchen floor. That success led to other jobs.

Few of Barnaby's shoots went smoothly. On one job, city-dog Barnaby was taken to the country. He had never seen cows and sheep before, but his instincts rescued him. Led to the cows, he had a fine time driving the startled herd past the cameras. For the next shot, sheep were brought in to replace the cows. Barnaby quickly ran forward to drive them. All at once, he stopped, sniffed, and shook his head. The sheep's damp, heavy wool smelled terrible. It was too much for Barnaby! Neither threats nor rewards could make him come close to that flock of smelly sheep.

Barnaby's greatest moment came in the film *Serpico*. He played the role of the hero's pet sheepdog. The film was shot in the summer, so fake snow had to be piled up for the winter scene. When Barnaby saw the snow, he was overjoyed. He jumped into the middle of a "snowdrift" and fake snow flew in all directions. In another scene, his owner was to get shot. Barnaby, watching from his place beside the director, couldn't bear to see his friend in pain. He trotted onto the set and licked the man's face. The "dying" man broke up and started giggling.

After *Serpico*, Barnaby had plenty of work. On set after set, he played silly games when he should have been working. Instead of firing him, directors were happy to rewrite their scripts to include his antics. After all Barnaby, like other Old English sheepdogs, was just having fun!

Old English sheepdogs are full of fun and mischief and enjoy playing with their owners.

▌GLOSSARY/INDEX

Bitch 33, 34—An adult female dog.

Breeding 8, 33—Mating a quality bitch to a quality male.

Canines 12—The four long, sharp fangs in the front of a dog's mouth.

Canker 31—An ear infection common in long-haired dogs.

Carnivore 8, 12—A meat-eating animal.

Choke Chain 25—A leash made from heavy metal links that is used in training a dog.

Crossbreed 9—To mate the offspring of two different breeds of dogs.

Dewclaws 34—Extra, useless claws that grow on the insides of a dog's legs. These are removed by a vet at the dog's birth.

Distemper 28—A serious disease that affects puppies.

Docking 9, 10—Shortening a dog's tail by cutting it off at the first or second joint.

Domestic Dog 8—Any member of the *canis familiaris* species that has been tamed for the use of human beings.

Gait 39—The movements of a dog's feet when it's walking, trotting, or galloping.

Grooming 18, 26, 27, 29, 30, 31, 32, 36, 39—Brushing a sheepdog to keep its coat from matting.

46

◢ GLOSSARY/INDEX

Haw 14—The dog's third eyelid.

Heat 22—The time when a bitch is ready to mate.

Hip Dysplasia 21, 28—An inherited condition that affects a dog's hip joints. A severe case can cripple an Old English sheepdog.

Hot Spot 32—A raw, itchy spot that forms on a long-haired dog's skin underneath the coat.

Housebreak 23—To train a puppy so it doesn't relieve itself inside the house.

Incisors 12—The cutting teeth that grow at the front of the dog's jaw between the canines.

Instincts 18, 23, 44—Natural behaviors that are inborn in a dog.

Litter 23, 34—A family of puppies born during a single whelping.

Molars 12—The dog's back teeth, used for chewing and grinding.

Obedience Trial 16—A competition in which the dog is judged on how well it follows its handler's commands.

Olfactory Patches 15—The nerve endings in the nose that provide a dog's keen sense of smell.

Pedigree 9, 22, 36—A chart that lists a dog's ancestors.

GLOSSARY/INDEX

Premolars 12—A dog's back teeth, used for slicing and chewing.

Puppy 10, 12, 13, 19, 20, 21, 22, 23, 24, 26, 28, 33, 34, 35, 36—A dog under one year of age.

Purebred 23, 33—A dog whose ancestors are all of the same breed.

Reinforce 25—To train a dog by giving it a reward when it obeys a command.

Show Dog 10, 11, 20, 30, 31—A dog that meets the highest standards of its breed.

Stud 33—A purebred male used for breeding.

Umbilical Cord 34—The hollow tube that carries nutrients to the puppy while it's inside the mother's body.

Veterinarian 15, 20, 22, 26, 27, 28, 32, 33, 34, 35, 36—A doctor who is trained to take care of animals.

Wean 23, 35, 36—To stop a puppy from nursing from its mother.

Whelping 34—The birth of a litter of puppies.

Withers 11, 12, 31—The dog's shoulder, the point where its neck joins the body. A dog's height is measured at the withers.

Worms 23, 28—Dangerous parasites that live in a dog's intestines.